T0386020

WiderWorld

POWERED BY

Practice
Tests Plus

EXAM PRACTICE
PEARSON TEST OF ENGLISH GENERAL **LEVEL 1**

Pearson Education Limited
Edinburgh Gate
Harlow
Essex CM20 2JE
and Associated Companies throughout the world.

The right of Liz Kilbey, Marta Umińska, Beata Trapnell, Rod Fricker and Kamil Petryk to be identified as authors of this Work has been asserted by them in accordance with the Copyright, Designs and Patents Act 1988.

First published 2016
ARP impression 98
ISBN: 978 1 292 14884 7

Set in Arial
Printed and bound by Ashford Colour Press Ltd

Acknowledgements

Material for Test 1 from authentic PTE General past papers
Material for Test 2 from *PTE General Skills Practice Level 1*, with revisions

The publisher would like to thank the following for their kind permission to reproduce their images:

(Key: b-bottom; c-centre; l-left; r-right; t-top)

Fotolia.com: 3ddock 25bl, 38br, art_vor 25cr, artisticco 26bl, 38tl, 38tc, 38tr, 38bl, 38bc, 40, 60l, 60c, 60r, ashva73 34l, Matthew Cole 33b, ComicVector 34c, Flo-Bo 26br, harvest 26bc, keko-ka 26c, macrovector 25c, Makkuro_GL 25bc, Neyro 25t, noppyviva 25cl, pisotskii 25br, raven, sbojanovic 34r, spinetta 32 (A, B), VKA 32 (A, C)

Illustrations by **Katerina Milusheva**: 6tc, 15t, 16b, 24, 26t, 27b, 33t, 34t, 42

All other images © Pearson Education Limited

Contents

There is no **Section 11** in PTE General Level 1.

Introduction

What is Pearson Test of English General?

PTE General is a suite of six tests at different levels (A1, 1, 2, 3, 4 and 5). It tests your ability in English in practical skills for real-life situations such as writing messages, understanding talks, understanding newspaper and magazine articles or taking part in conversations. PTE General tests are taken three times a year in May, June and December in centres all around the world.

The tests do not assume any experience of work or knowledge of the world and so are most suitable for teenagers and young adults who expect to use English in their future academic and professional lives.

Key Features

The sections and items in PTE General Level 1 are grouped together into themes or topics related to familiar and routine matters such as the home, the family, work, shopping, education, travel and entertainment. The listening and reading texts are specially written so that the level sounds authentic. The four skills – listening, speaking, reading and writing – are tested in an integrated way. For example, you listen to some information and write about what you have heard, or you read a text and then answer questions or complete notes based on what you have read.

Test Structure

PTE General is divided into two parts – the Written Test and the Spoken Test.

The Written Test

The Written Test of PTE General consists of nine sections and takes 1 hour and 35 minutes at Level 1.

Section 1: Listening

Section 1 consists of ten short listening texts – monologues and dialogues. Each text is followed by a question and three possible picture options. You must choose the correct answer by putting a cross (✗) in a box. There is a short pause before each recording for you to look at the pictures before you listen, and another pause after the recording for you to choose which of the three pictures matches what you have heard. This section tests your ability to understand the main idea of what someone says. You will hear the recording only once.

Section 2: Listening and Writing

Section 2 is a dictation. You will hear one person speaking and you must write down exactly what you hear with the correct spelling. You will hear the recording twice, the second time with pauses to give you time to write. The passage can be a news broadcast, an announcement, instructions or factual information.

Section 3: Listening

In Section 3, you will hear two listening texts, including conversations, announcements and recorded messages. You have to complete notes for each listening using the information you have heard. There are five gaps to fill for each listening text. This section may test your ability to understand and write down detailed information including addresses, telephone numbers and website addresses. You will hear each text twice.

Section 4: Reading

In Section 4, you read five short texts, each containing a gap, and you choose which of three possible answers is the missing word or phrase that fills the gap. This section tests your ability to understand specific information and/or the overall meaning of the text. The reading texts can be instructions, signs, notices, labels, advertisements, menus or announcements.

Section 5: Reading

In Section 5, you read five short texts and for each one you choose one picture which matches the text from a choice of three. This section tests your understanding of the main idea of a text. The reading texts can give descriptions or directions, and the pictures can include maps or diagrams.

Section 6: Reading

There are two reading texts in this section. Each text is followed by four questions for you to answer using a word or a short phrase. They test your understanding of the main points of the texts. The types of reading can be letters, emails, articles from newspapers or magazines, leaflets, brochures or website articles.

Section 7: Reading

In Section 7, you read a text and use the information to fill in seven gaps in sentences or a set of notes. This section tests your understanding of specific detailed information you have read. The reading text can be an email, a letter, an advertisement, a newspaper or magazine article, or a section from a website or textbook.

Section 8: Writing

Section 8 is a writing test. You have to write a piece of correspondence – an email, a formal or an informal letter, a postcard or notes – based on the information that you have read in Section 7. At Level 1, you have to write 50–70 words.

Section 9: Writing

In Section 9, you will be asked to write a text based on a series of pictures. There are two options to choose from. Each option consists of a series of three images/pictures. The text to write at Level 1 is 80–100 words long. You will be asked to write a short story, a description or a diary entry.

The Spoken Test

The Spoken Test of PTE General consists of three sections (Sections 10, 12 and 13) and takes 5 minutes at Level 1.

Section 10: Speaking

In the first part of the Test, the examiner will ask you a question and you have to talk about yourself for about a minute. You will talk about your interests and hobbies, the sports you take part in, the films or books you like, etc. The examiner may ask you further questions to find out more information.

Section 11: Speaking

There is no discussion section at Level 1.

Section 12: Speaking

In Section 12, you will be shown a picture and asked to describe it. You will be asked to describe people, interiors (for example, a home, a school, a shop, a restaurant), public places (for example, a street or a park) and everyday activities. You will have about 2 minutes to do this.

Section 13: Speaking

The final section of the Spoken Test is a role play. You will be given a card with details of your role and some instructions. The role play includes situations such as shopping, ordering food and drink, public transportation and asking for directions. This section of the test takes about 1.5 minutes.

Exam Practice: PTE General

The *Exam Practice: PTE General* series has been specially written to help you become familiar with the format and content of the PTE General Test. They contain two full practice tests, plus exam and writing guide sections to help you to improve your general level of English as well as your score in the test. Level 1 contains:

- Two *Practice Tests* for both the Written and Spoken Tests, the first of which has tips giving advice on how to deal with specific questions, or aspects of questions.

- An *Exam Guide* with advice on how to approach each section and deal with particular problems that might occur.

- A *Writing Guide* which concentrates on the writing tasks you will meet in the tests, giving example answers, writing tips and useful language.

Practice Test 1 with Guidance

Section 1

You will have 10 seconds to read each question. Listen and put a cross (✗) in the box next to the correct answer, as in the example. You have 10 seconds to choose the correct option.

Example: What does Anna want to buy?

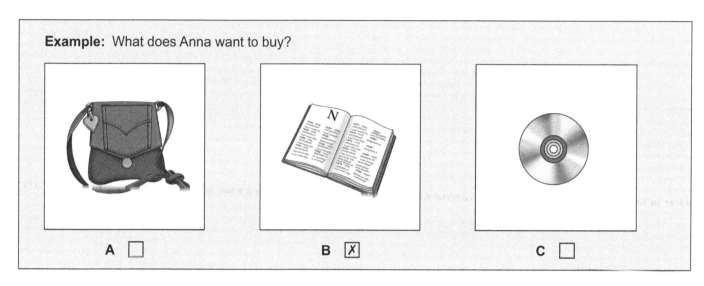

A ☐   B ☒   C ☐

---

1. What is the woman's job?

A ☐   B ☐   C ☐

---

2. Which is Elizabeth's bike?

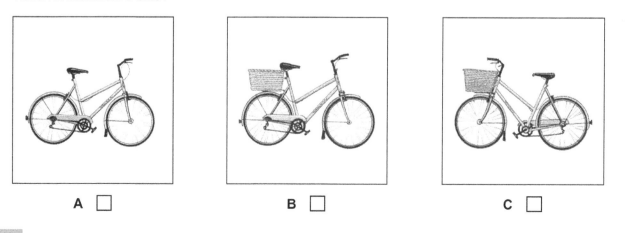

A ☐   B ☐   C ☐

3. Who is the message for?

A ☐

B ☐

C ☐

4. How is the man going to the station?

A ☐

B ☐

C ☐

5. Which is the correct picture?

A ☐

B ☐

C ☐

6. What's the boy doing this afternoon?

A ☐

B ☐

C ☐

7. What is Mr Hammond's job?

A ☐

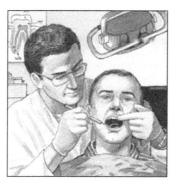
B ☐

C ☐

8. Where's the sandwich?

A ☐

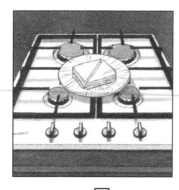
B ☐

C ☐

9. What is Julia going to do that morning?

A ☐

B ☐

C ☐

10. Which platform is the train to York leaving from?

A ☐

B ☐

C ☐

Tip strip
6: What isn't the boy doing today? What's the weather like?
9: Listen for a time in the morning.

11. You will hear a recording about pets. Listen to the whole recording once. Then you will hear the recording again with pauses for you to write down what you hear. Make sure you spell the words correctly.

Tip strip
- Listen carefully and try to use your knowledge of grammar to get the endings right.
- If you miss a word, don't worry. Try to keep up. You can go back and guess the missing word from the context before you move on to the next section.
- Don't forget to check your grammar and spelling when you have finished.

Section 3

12–16 You will hear a voicemail message. First, read the notes below, then listen and complete the notes with information from the voicemail. You will hear the recording twice.

> **Example:** Message from: _Nick_

12. Day when Nick moves: ....

13. Time Angie needs to arrive: ....

14. Angie must take: ....

15. Angie can help Nick: ....

16. Nick's new number: 07849 ....

17–21 You will hear a telephone message. First, read the notes below, then listen and complete the notes with information from the telephone message. You will hear the recording twice.

> **Example:** Name of vet's: _The Ark_

17. Tel. no: ....

18. Morning opening: 8.30 – ....

19. Dog's name: ....

20. Best time for appointment: ....

21. If today, send: ....

Tip strip

12: You are listening for when Nick needs help.
14: Listen carefully. What does Nick want Angie to bring with her?

17: The speaker gives a telephone number – write the numbers you hear.
18: Be careful. You are listening for the closing time of the clinic.
20: Listen for the time he prefers to have the appointment.

Section 4

Read each text and put a cross (X) by the missing word or phrase, as in the example.

Example:

> Sightseeing tours depart from the bus station
> on the hour .... from 10.00 to 18.00.
> Tickets – $20 for adults and $10 for children.

A ☐ sometimes
B ☒ every hour
C ☐ in the mornings

22.

> ## School Trip
>
> Do you want to go to France next month?
> Then .... your name on this list.

A ☐ put
B ☐ see
C ☐ take

23.

> A Dayrider bus ticket allows you to use the
> city buses .... as you wish during the
> course of the day.

A ☐ as well
B ☐ as many times
C ☐ as cheaply

24.

> # Gino's Restaurant
>
> We are looking for the following staff:
> ### Manager
> ### Cook
> ....
> ### Cleaner
> Tel: **01202 687213** for further details

A ☐ Customer

B ☐ Waiter

C ☐ Shop assistant

25.

> ### Notice to all Food Workers
>
> .... , cover it and wear gloves at all times.
>
> *Mike Morrison*
> *Health and Safety Manager*

A ☐ Tie your hair back

B ☐ Wear a uniform

C ☐ Be clean and fresh

26.

> *Notice:* You are approaching passport control.
> Go straight ahead. Please have your passport
> ready for ....

A ☐ inspection

B ☐ recommendation

C ☐ arrival

Tip strip

23: Think about what you can do with the ticket. What is the advantage of a Dayrider ticket?

25: Which option mentions something you should cover when working with food?

26: Think about what happens at the airport. What do they do with your passport?

Section 5

For each question, put a cross (✗) in the box below the correct picture, as in the example.

Example:

The Desert by Jane Green is the latest of her wonderful films set in Africa. It's on at the Regal until the end of this week, but after that you'll have to go to the Majestic. Or, of course, you can rent the DVD from The Film Centre.

Which cinema is showing *The Desert* next week?

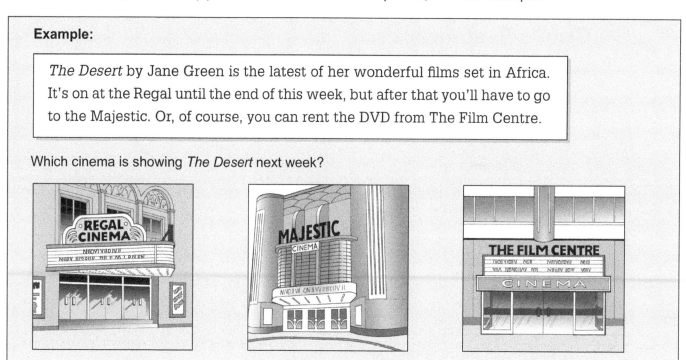

A ☐   B ☒   C ☐

27.

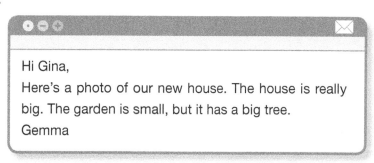

Hi Gina,
Here's a photo of our new house. The house is really big. The garden is small, but it has a big tree.
Gemma

Which is the correct picture?

A ☐   B ☐   C ☐

28.

Dear Customers,
We are now in a new place in the Arnedale District. Take a left in Duke Drive opposite the bowling alley and then the second right. Go past the supermarket. Our new shop is next to Clegg's garage.

Maxine's Pets

Where is Maxine's Pets?

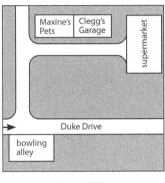

A ☐

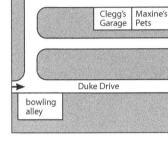

B ☐

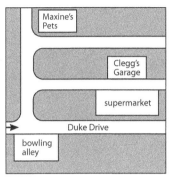

C ☐

29.

Going on holiday and need new luggage?
Check out the new Easypull Case.
Light and easy to pull along with front and back wheels. Black only.
A bargain at £20.00.

Which is the new Easypull case?

A ☐

B ☐

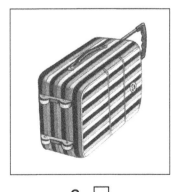

C ☐

Tip strip
28: Look carefully for what is 'next to' Maxine's Pets.
29: Does the Easypull case have wheels? What colours are available?

30.

> ### Italian restaurant
> ### NEEDS HELP IN THE KITCHEN
> on Friday and Saturday evenings, 5–10.
> Preparing fruit and vegetables for the chef.
> No cooking, cleaning or waiting on tables.

Which picture shows the job?

A ☐   B ☐   C ☐

31.

> ### Bus Information
> From this bus stop, buses run to the city centre every ten minutes
> starting at 6.00 a.m. and finishing at 11.30 p.m.
> Single fare 75p. Return £1.20.

When is the last bus of the day?

A ☐   B ☐   C ☐

Tip strip

30: What <u>doesn't</u> the job include?

Section 6

Read the advertisement below and answer the questions.

Have a great holiday weekend at
Compton Farm Activity Centre, North Wales

You can choose activities such as climbing, hill-walking and hang-gliding.
We are also near the coast and offer sailing and diving lessons.
Adventure for all ages. *(We have people in their eighties!)*

- ○ Accommodation and all meals at Compton Farm.
- ○ Choose your activities online.
- ○ 10 percent off when you book twelve weeks before.

Example: Where is Compton Farm Activity Centre? *North Wales*

---

32. What water activities can you do there? ....

33. How old must you be to go there? ....

34. Where do you sleep and eat? ....

35. How can you get a cheaper holiday weekend? ....

Read the information below and answer the questions.

❖ You can visit **Berry Castle** in the small town of Berrisford. It was built 800 years ago and it is in very good condition today. The castle is open to visitors from 1st April to 31st October. There is no car park for Berry Castle, but you can use the town centre car park. This year, for the first time, a restaurant is now open in the gardens of the castle. Castle entry £10.00. Half price for children under fourteen.

Example: Where is Berry Castle? *Berrisford*

---

36. How old is it? ....

37. From the beginning of which month is the castle closed? ....

38. Where can you park? ....

39. What is new this year? ....

Tip strip

40: Which is the first month the castle is open?

41: This is the amount of time you need for a visit to the castle.

43: You are looking for a date when the boat hire is not available.

46: You are looking for a place where you can take photographs.

Read the brochure and complete the notes. Write **no more than three words** in each gap from the brochure.

Visiting
Buntleigh Castle and Gardens

Buntleigh Castle and gardens are open from April to October. The castle is home to one of the world's largest collections of butterflies. Children's attractions include an adventure playground and model railway. There is a lot to see and do, so we suggest you allow about four hours for your visit.

On the lake, boats are available for hire from 12 a.m. until 4 p.m. and cost £10.00. Please note that on 20th August there will be no boats for hire as the lake is being used for a film shoot.

Audio guides are available from the Ticket Office in English or French. Price £4.00.

Other information: Toilets are situated at the Lakeside Restaurant. Parking is £2.50 per vehicle. Photography is not allowed in the castle, but is permitted in the gardens. Dogs are permitted in the grounds.

Example: Name of the castle: _Buntleigh_

---

40. Earliest month you can visit the castle: ....

41. Suggested time you spend at the castle: ....

42. Price of boat hire: ....

43. When the lake is closed to the public: ....

44. Where you can get an audio guide: ....

45. Cost to park your car: ....

46. Photography is allowed: ....

Use the information in **Section 7** to help you write your answer.

Tip strip

- Choose information from the Section 7 text that relates to what you are asked to do, but use your own language and do not copy large parts from the text.
- Make sure that you include all the points from the exam task and that you write between 50 and 70 words.
- When you have finished, remember to check your work for spelling and grammar.

47. You have read the brochure about Buntleigh Castle. Now write an email to a friend. **Write 50 to 70 words** and include the following information:

- tell him/her about Buntleigh Castle
- tell him/her what you can do there
- suggest that you go to visit the castle together

Use your own words.

Section 9

48. Choose **one** of the topics below and write your answer in **80–100 words**.

A Jessie is your friend. He had some trouble walking his dog. Look at the pictures and write a short story about how he solved his problem.

B Write a diary entry about your birthday party last night and what happened the next day.

Tip strip

- Before you choose the topic, think about the vocabulary you will need to use in your text.
- Make a short, rough plan of the ideas you want to include and note down any key words.
- Don't forget to check your grammar and spelling when you have finished writing, and that you have written between 80 and 100 words.

Section 10 (1.5 minutes)

In this section you will speak on your own for about a minute. Listen to what your teacher/examiner asks. Your teacher/examiner will ask one of the main questions below, and the follow-up questions if necessary.

Preliminary prompt 1: *Do you enjoy music?*

Main prompt 1: *Tell me the type of music you enjoy listening to.*

Follow-up prompts:
- *Where do you usually listen to music?*
- *Do you know any songs in English?*
- *What's the most popular music in your country?*
- *How often do you buy CDs?*

Preliminary prompt 2: *What time do you usually have dinner?*

Main prompt 2: *Tell me what happens at dinnertime in your house.*

Follow-up prompts:
- *Who usually does the cooking?*
- *What's a typical meal for your family?*
- *Where do you have dinner?*
- *Which is your favourite meal? Why?*

Preliminary prompt 3: *Do you enjoy school?*

Main prompt 3: *Tell me about the best day of the week at school. (For test takers at school)*

Follow-up prompts:
- *What do you do on that day?*
- *Are there any days you really dislike? Why?*
- *How long is your schoolday?*
- *What is your favourite subject? Why?*

Preliminary prompt 4: *Do you enjoy work?*

Main prompt 4: *Tell me about the best day of the week at work? (For test takers at work)*

Follow-up prompts:
- *What usually happens on that day?*
- *Are there any days you really dislike? Why?*
- *How long is your working day?*
- *What part of your job do you enjoy most?*

Tip strip
- Remember it is quite natural to pause very briefly for thought when you are speaking.
- When the examiner asks you follow-up questions, try to avoid one-word answers.

There is no **Section 11** in PTE General Level 1.

In this section you will talk about the picture for up to 1 minute. Your teacher/examiner will say:

Please tell me what you can see and what is happening in the picture.

Tell your teacher/examiner what you can see and what is happening in the picture.

Your teacher/examiner may ask you some of the following questions if necessary:

*   *How many girls can you see?*
*   *What are the people wearing?*
*   *How old are the people?*
*   *Who are these people?*
*   *What do you think has just happened?*

Tip strip

• If you find you can't remember (or don't know) the right word for something, don't worry – try to get round the problem by saying something like: *I can't remember what it's called but it's one of those things for ...-ing.*

In this section you will take part in a role play. Your teacher/examiner will explain the situation.

Test taker's card

You are on a football field. You invite your friend to play on your team. The examiner is your friend.

- Greet your friend.
- Say you want him/her to play on your football team.
- Tell him/her why you want him/her to play on your football team.
- Invite him/her to play on your football team tomorrow.

Your teacher/examiner is your friend. Below is a sample script that your teacher/examiner may use.

We are on a football field. I am your friend and you are inviting me to play on your team.

Ready? You start.

- *Hello/Good morning/Good afternoon*
- *Why do you want me to play on your football team?*
- *I can't play today because I must go home.*
- *Yes, I'd love to play football with you tomorrow.*

Thank you. That is the end of the test.

Tip strip

- What would you say in real life in this situation? Take time to understand the situation and just be as natural as possible.

Practice Test 2

Section 1

You will have 10 seconds to read each question. Listen and put a cross (**✗**) in the box next to the correct answer, as in the example. You have 10 seconds to choose the correct option.

Example: What does Anna want to buy?

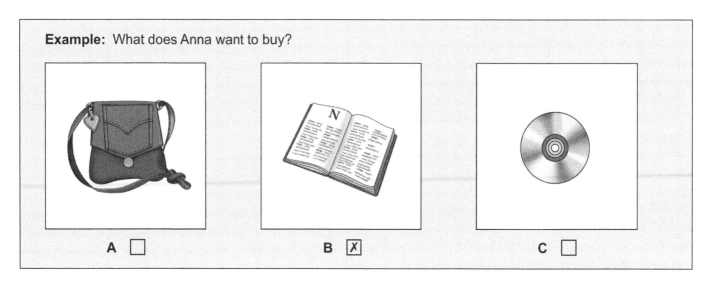

A ☐   B ✗   C ☐

---

1. What was Ben doing last night?

A ☐   B ☐   C ☐

---

2. Who is the speaker describing?

A ☐   B ☐   C ☐

3. What is next to the Majestic?

A ☐

B ☐

C ☐

4. Who is the man talking about?

A ☐

B ☐

C ☐

5. Where are the speakers?

A ☐

B ☐

C ☐

6. What's her job?

 **A** ☐

 **B** ☐

 **C** ☐

7. Where is Tom?

 **A** ☐

 **B** ☐

 **C** ☐

8. Where do they go on holiday?

 **A** ☐

 **B** ☐

 **C** ☐

9. What is Josh using?

A ☐

B ☐

C ☐

10. What is he describing?

A ☐

B ☐

C ☐

11. You will hear a recording about Ann's grandfather. Listen to the whole recording once. Then you will hear the recording again with pauses for you to write down what you hear. Make sure you spell the words correctly.

Section 3

12–16 You will hear an advertisement. First, read the notes below, then listen and complete the notes with information from the advertisement. You will hear the recording twice.

> **Example:** Advertisement for: *a shopping centre*

12. Number of shops: ....

13. What children do in the learning centre: ....

14. Cost of using the learning centre: ....

15. On Sundays, the centre closes at: ....

16. Free shopper's bus from: ....

17–21 You will hear a presentation about the Eiffel Tower. First, read the notes below then listen and complete the notes with information from the presentation. You will hear the recording twice.

> **Example:** Number of tourists who visit the Eiffel Tower every year: *7 million*

17. The tower is .... old.

18. The shape of the base: ....

19. How often it is painted: ....

20. How you go from the second floor to the third level: ....

21. How to buy tickets to avoid queuing: ....

Section 4

Read each text and put a cross (✗) by the missing word or phrase, as in the example.

Example:

> ### *Mountain Walking Club*
> *Do you like walking in the mountains?*
> *Are you looking for new friends?*
> .... the walking club for free! This month only!
> *Fridays 5 p.m.–7 p.m.*
> *All welcome!*

A ☐ Be

B ☒ Join

C ☐ Go

22.

> We are sorry to inform you that the vending
> machine is temporarily out of ....
> Please use another one.

A ☐ work

B ☐ order

C ☐ run

23.

> Come to Dartmoor, one of England's most mysterious places.
> You can stop in the many parking areas, admire .... and
> see some rare birds.

A ☐ the cars

B ☐ the views

C ☐ the food

24.

> ☀ **Clean Up** is looking for fit, strong adults with their own .... who can spend a few hours during the week or weekend collecting unwanted electrical equipment.

A ☐ cups

B ☐ furniture

C ☐ transport

25.

> # SUSIE'S
> **is a clothes shop with .... !**
> **You won't find anything boring here.**

A ☐ a difference

B ☐ a place

C ☐ an area

26.

> In this supermarket the prices
> will always be lower than any other shop.
> If you find the same thing cheaper,
> you will get your .... back.

A ☐ receipt

B ☐ money

C ☐ shopping

Section 5

For each question, put a cross (X) in the box below the correct picture, as in the example.

Example:

The Desert by Jane Green is the latest of her wonderful films set in Africa. It's on at the Regal until the end of this week, but after that you'll have to go to the Majestic. Or, of course, you can rent the DVD from The Film Centre.

Which cinema is showing *The Desert* next week?

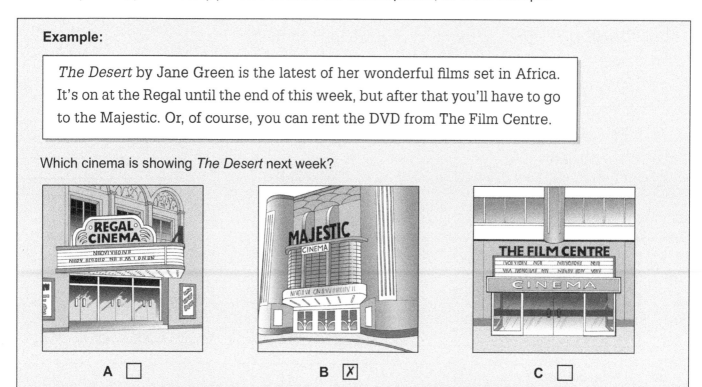

A ☐   B ☒   C ☐

27.

This is a picture of Henry. He's got short dark hair and lovely dark eyes. I think he usually wears glasses. He needs them for reading, but he isn't wearing them in the photo. The only thing wrong is his hat. I think he'd definitely look better without it!

What is Henry wearing in the photo?

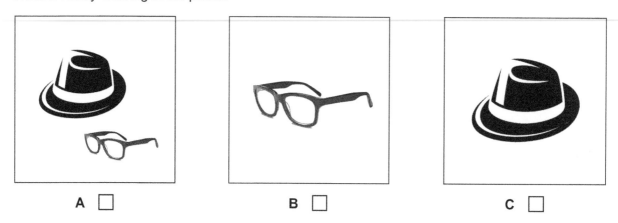

A ☐   B ☐   C ☐

28.

> Our café is busy with food orders from people who work in shops and offices nearby, and we need help. You need to be honest, fast and friendly! You will deliver the orders by bicycle for two hours daily. This job is perfect for university students with some free time.

What will you use in this job?

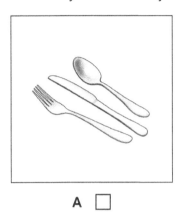

A ☐

B ☐

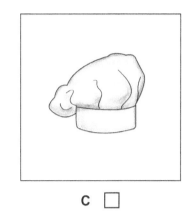

C ☐

29.

> We can do different sports at the sports club in my school. I wanted to do basketball, but there aren't any places left in the team. I think I'll do karate – the coach said that I'm quite good at it. The first class is tomorrow.

What sport is Mark going to do?

A ☐

B ☐

C ☐

30.

The bank is not far from here, it is just a short walk. You need to go down the road, and past the post office. Then turn left. You will see the bank on the left, it is opposite the library.

Which is the correct map?

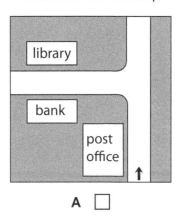

A ☐

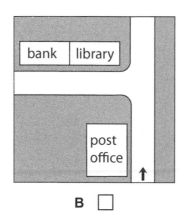

B ☐

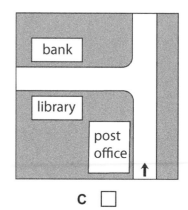

C ☐

31.

Kirk often travels in the summer with his backpack to discover new locations, especially in Asia and Europe. He likes taking photographs, meeting new people, talking to them and getting to know their culture, food and languages. He's planning his next trip to relax.

What activity does Kirk enjoy when he is on holiday?

A ☐

B ☐

C ☐

Section 6

Read the email below and answer the questions.

Hi Mark,

There's a concert in London next month. I have bought two tickets, but Jane is going on a business trip and can't go with me. Would you like to go? We need to get there the night before and I have booked a room at Bird Lodge. First, I wanted to drive down, but then I got very cheap train tickets, so you don't need to do anything at all. It would be fun to go together.

Chris

Example: When is the concert going to be? _Next month_

32. Why can't Jane go? ....

33. When should they arrive there? ....

34. Where are they going to stay? ....

35. How are they going to travel? ....

Read the story about a holiday below and answer the questions.

Last spring my parents wanted to spend some time far from the noisy city where we live. They used the Internet to book a nice cottage in the countryside. When we got to the cottage, we were really disappointed. The house was next to a busy road. There were too many cars. Then the cooker didn't work. And at night we were terribly cold because we only had thin blankets.

We were really glad to return home the following day!

Example: Where did the parents want to go? _Far from the noisy city_

36. Where did the parents look for the place? ....

37. When they got to the house, where was it? ....

38. What was the problem with the cooker? ....

39. Why were they cold at night? ....

Section 7

Read the information about a hotel and complete the notes. Write **no more than three words** in each gap from the text.

> # Come to the NEPTUNE HOTEL
>
> The Neptune Hotel is a 216-room hotel in one of Bulgaria's best known and most beautiful resorts. It is situated 200 metres from the Black Sea on a golden sandy beach and 400 metres from the centre of the town with its excellent restaurants and great nightlife.
>
> You'll feel like a king (or a queen) here. You will have some amazing forty-five square metres to relax in. There's a flat-screen TV with satellite channels and free Wi-Fi Internet. There is a large balcony with a view of the sea where you can have breakfast if you wish and, of course, a king-sized bed.
>
> There is something for everyone at the Neptune. The fun and games start straight after breakfast at 11 a.m. and continue until long after dinner. There are tours, water sports, quizzes and discos. We also organise performances by local singers and dancers.

Example: Hotel name: _Neptune_

40. Country: ....

41. Distance to the sea: ....

42. Type of beach: ....

43. Room size: ....

44. Type of a TV in the room: ....

45. View from the room: ....

46. The fun and games finish: ....

Section 8

Use the information in **Section 7** to help you write your answer.

47. Write a postcard to your friend and tell him/her about your stay at the Neptune Hotel. **Write 50 to 70 words** and include the following information:

- tell him/her where the hotel is
- tell him/her what the hotel is like
- tell him/her what you have done during the holiday

Use your own words.

Section 9

48. Choose **one** of the topics below and write your answer in **80–100 words**.

    A Yesterday, your father had a holiday from work. Look at the pictures and write a description of what you and your father did together for your diary.

    B You and your family had a good time last weekend. Look at the pictures and write about it.

Section 10 (1.5 minutes)

In this section you will speak on your own for about a minute. Listen to what your teacher/examiner asks. Your teacher/examiner will ask one of the main questions below and the follow-up questions if necessary.

Preliminary prompt 1: *Do you have many friends?*

Main prompt 1: *Tell me about one of your close friends.*

Follow-up prompts:
- *What do you usually do with your friends?*
- *How often do you talk to your friends?*
- *Where do you usually meet your friends?*
- *Do you make friends easily? Why/Why not?*

Preliminary prompt 2: *How important are computers to you?*

Main prompt 2: *Tell me about technology in your life.*

Follow-up prompts:
- *Do you use a computer for work/school/college?*
- *When did you first start using a computer?*
- *What do you use a computer for?*
- *Are you good at using computers?*

Preliminary prompt 3: *Do you have a mobile phone?*

Main prompt 3: *Tell me how you use your mobile phone.*

Follow-up prompts:
- *Who do you call or text most often?*
- *How many texts do you send every day?*
- *When did you get your first phone?*
- *Could you live without your phone?*

Preliminary prompt 4: *Do you like your local area?*

Main prompt 4: *Tell me about the area you live in.*

Follow-up prompts:
- *What do you usually buy in your local shop?*
- *Do you feel safe in the area where you live?*
- *Is your neighbourhood busy?*
- *How long does it take you to travel from home to work/school?*

There is no **Section 11** in PTE General Level 1.

Section 12 (2 minutes)

In this section you will talk about the picture for up to 1 minute. Your teacher/examiner will say:

Please tell me what you can see and what is happening in the picture.

Tell your teacher/examiner what you can see and what is happening in the picture.

Your teacher/examiner may ask you some of the following questions if necessary:
* *Where are they?*
* *What are they using?*
* *What is the man doing?*
* *What is he wearing?*
* *What can you see on the table?*

Section 13 (1.5 minutes)

In this section you will take part in a role play. Your teacher/examiner will explain the situation.

> **Test taker's card**
>
> You are in a travel agency to book a holiday in India.
> The examiner is the travel agent.
>
> - Say what you want
> - Say when you want to go
> - Say how long you want to go for
> - Ask for the price of the holiday
> - Thank the travel agent

Your teacher/examiner is the travel agent. Below is a sample script that your teacher/examiner may use.

We are in a travel agency. I am the travel agent and you want to book a holiday in India.

Ready? I'll start.

- *Hello, how can I help you?*
- *When do you want to go?*
- *How long do you want to be away for?*
- *That's fine.*
- *It's £1,350 per person.*
- *No problem.*

Thank you. That is the end of the test.

Exam Guide

Section 1: Graphical multiple choice

What is being tested?

Section 1 tests your ability to understand the main idea of a short spoken text.

What do you have to do?

Answer ten questions. For each question, you will listen to a short recording. You will hear each recording once. For each one, you will see a question and three possible picture options (A, B and C). You have to listen to the recording and the question and decide which picture answers the question best.

- Read and listen to the instructions.

- For each question, you will have 10 seconds to read the question and check the picture options. Pictures can sometimes look very similar; think about what is different in each picture.

- Remember that you have only one chance to listen.

- Put a cross in the box next to the picture you think answers the question best.

- The questions are marked as either correct or incorrect. If you are not sure, choose the picture you think is most likely – you may be right.

- Try to get used to hearing a range of voices and accents. Search online for an English language radio programme on a topic that interests you. You won't understand every word, but listen and try to get the key ideas as you listen.

The amount of time to read before you listen.

How you answer.

You will have 10 seconds to read each question. Listen and put a cross (**X**) in the box next to the correct answer, as in the example. You have 10 seconds to choose the correct option.

The amount of time to answer after you listen.

Pay attention to the question word.

The man asks if she is going to buy a bag or a CD, but she says "No! I want to get a new dictionary."

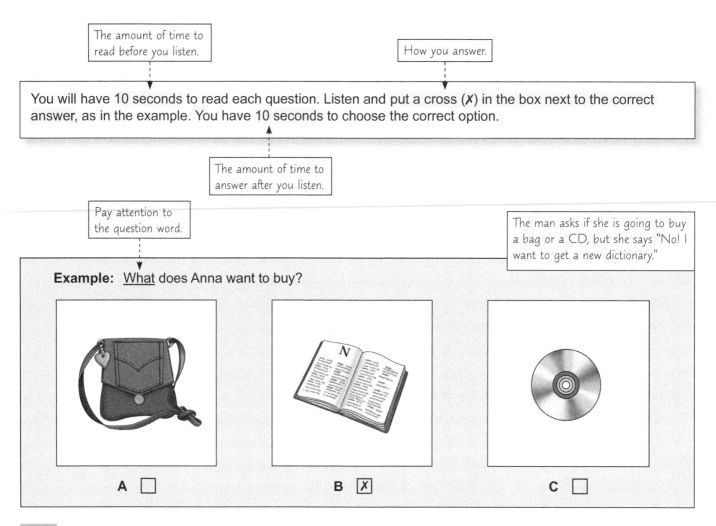

Example: <u>What</u> does Anna want to buy?

A ☐   B ☒   C ☐

Section 2: Dictation

What is being tested?

Section 2 assesses listening and writing skills. It tests your ability to understand an extended piece of speech by transcribing a spoken text.

What do you have to do?

Listen to one person speaking and write exactly what you hear with correct spellings. You will hear the recording twice; the second time with pauses, giving you time to write down word-for-word what you hear. There is one dictation to complete and therefore only one recording.

Strategy

- Read and listen to the instructions.
- Pay attention to the topic of the recording.
- During the first reading of the dictation, listen very carefully to the whole recording. The subject is always given in the instructions. Try to understand the overall extract and pick out some key words. If you write the key words as you hear them, you will have a better chance of recognising the topic vocabulary and words that go together.
- You will hear the recording for a second time. This time with pauses giving you time to write the words down.
- If you miss or misunderstand a word during the second listening, leave a space and keep writing. When the dictation has finished, read it through and use your knowledge of the topic vocabulary and grammar to help you guess the missing words. If what you have written down doesn't make sense, then you have probably misheard it, so consider changing it to something that sounds similar and makes sense.
- Check you have spelt the words correctly.

Preparation tips

- Improve your general listening skills: practise listening to a topic and understanding the main ideas. Search online for an English language radio programme on a topic that interests you or for public announcements:
  - You won't understand every word, but listen and try to note down the key words as you listen.
  - Practise picking out the key words; these are usually words that the speaker stresses.
  - Practise listening and writing the key words down at the same time.
  - Use your knowledge of grammar to get word endings right.

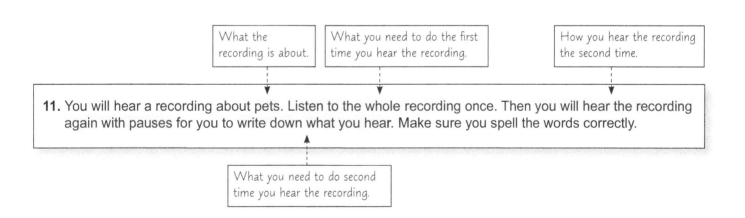

| What the recording is about. | What you need to do the first time you hear the recording. | How you hear the recording the second time. |

11. You will hear a recording about pets. Listen to the whole recording once. Then you will hear the recording again with pauses for you to write down what you hear. Make sure you spell the words correctly.

| What you need to do second time you hear the recording. |

Section 3: Text, note completion

What is being tested?

Section 3 tests your ability to extract specific information from extended spoken texts.

What do you have to do?

Listen to two recordings, and complete notes or sentences for each using the information you have heard. There are ten gaps to complete; five per task. You will hear each recording twice.

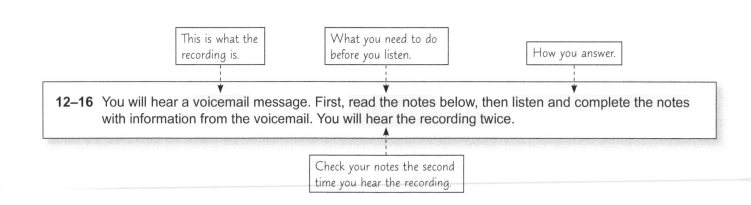

This is what the recording is.

What you need to do before you listen.

How you answer.

12–16 You will hear a voicemail message. First, read the notes below, then listen and complete the notes with information from the voicemail. You will hear the recording twice.

Check your notes the second time you hear the recording.

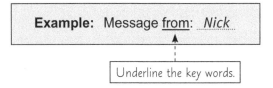

Example: Message <u>from</u>: *Nick*

Underline the key words.

Section 4: Gap fill 3-option multiple choice

What is being tested?

Section 4 tests your ability to understand the main idea of short written texts.

What do you have to do?

Answer five questions. Read five short texts, each containing a gap, and choose which one out of three answer options is the missing word or phrase. There are five gaps to complete; one per text.

- Read the instructions carefully.
- Read each question and the three options carefully and highlight any key words. Think about what is different in each option.
- When you have chosen your answer, check the other options again to make sure they cannot be correct.
- Re-read the text with your selected option to check that the text makes sense (in terms of meaning). If it doesn't, you will need to review your answer.

- Do as many practice tests as possible so that you fully understand the task and what you should do.
- Ask yourself what type of text it is and why it was written.
- Practise underlining the keys words in the text and using this information to consider the meaning of the missing words. You can practise this by working with a partner: choose one text each, remove some words from the text, and then swap them. Underline the key words and try to understand what information is missing.
- Keep a vocabulary notebook in which you write down useful vocabulary you come across, arranged by topic.
- When you learn a new word, write down not only the word, but also the sentence it is used in.

| How you answer. |

Read each text and put a cross (✗) by the missing word or phrase, as in the example.

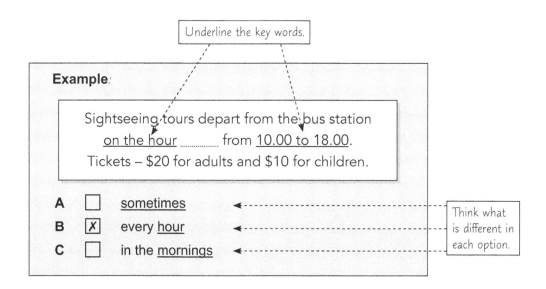

| Underline the key words. |

Example:

Sightseeing tours depart from the bus station
on the hour .... from 10.00 to 18.00.
Tickets – $20 for adults and $10 for children.

A ☐ sometimes
B ☒ every hour ← Think what is different in each option.
C ☐ in the mornings

Section 5: 3-option graphical multiple choice

What is being tested?

Section 5 tests your ability to understand the main idea of a short written text.

What do you have to do?

Read five short texts. There is a question for each text and three picture options. Choose the picture that answers the question best.

Strategy

- Before you read each text, look at the pictures carefully so you are clear what each one shows and how they are different.
- Read the text and underline the key words.
- Then look at the pictures and choose the one that answers the question best.
- Check the other options to make sure they don't match.

Preparation tips

- Do as many practice tests as possible so that you fully understand the task and what you should do.
- Read as much as you can in your free time. The reading that you do outside the classroom will help you become a better reader.

> How you answer.

For each question, put a cross (✗) in the box below the correct picture, as in the example.

> Underline the key words and information in the text.

> The film is only on at the Regal "until the end of this week", so the correct answer is B: "after that you'll have to go to the Majestic."

Example:

The Desert by Jane Green is the latest of her wonderful films set in Africa. It's on 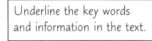 at the Regal until the end of this week, but after that you'll have to go to the Majestic. Or, of course, you can rent the DVD from The Film Centre.

Which cinema is showing *The Desert* next week?

A ☐   B ☒   C ☐

> Underline the key words in the question.

Section 6: Open-ended question

What is being tested?

Section 6 tests your ability to understand the main points of short written texts.

What do you have to do?

Read two texts and answer eight questions about them using single words or short answers. There are eight questions to answer; four per text.

Strategy

- Before you read the text, read the questions and focus on the key words. These are often questions words such as *what, why, how, when*.

- Pay attention to the key words, they will tell you exactly what information you need to find.

- Try to answer each question briefly and accurately using words from the text where appropriate.

- Try to avoid writing long answers with unnecessary information. Your answer doesn't have to be written as a sentence – often a word or phrase is enough.

- To help you focus your thoughts, underline or highlight the area in the text where you think the answer is.

Preparation tips

- Do as many practice tests as possible so that you fully understand the task and what you should do.

- Remember that Pearson Test of English General aims to test real-life skills. The reading that you do outside the classroom will help you become a better reader.

- Practise reading texts quickly all the way through to understand the main ideas. You could read notices in newspapers, magazines or online, and summarise the main ideas in them, even if you don't know all the vocabulary.

What you do.

Read the advertisement below and answer the questions.

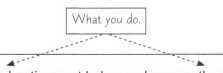

Example: <u>Where</u> is Compton Farm Activity Centre? *North Wales*

Read the questions and underline the question word and the key words before you read the text. Here, the question word tells you the answer is a place.

Section 7: Text, note completion

What is being tested?

Section 7 tests your ability to extract specific information from an extended written text.

What do you have to do?

Read a text and use information from it to fill gaps in seven incomplete sentences or notes. You must use no more than three words from the text to do this. There are seven sentences or notes to complete and one source text.

<table>
<tr><td>

Strategy

- Before you read the text, read the questions carefully and highlight or underline the key words.
- Scan the passage for the information or detail that is missing from the questions.
- When you read the text, you may find the same key word or a synonym of the key word in the text. Use the key words to decide what word or words are needed.
- Remember to use no more than three words from the text to complete the sentence or note.
- Check that your completed sentence makes sense and is grammatically correct.
- Read through all your answers before going to the next section.

</td><td>

Preparation tips

- Do as many practice tests as possible so that you fully understand the task and what you should do.
- Remember that Pearson Test of English General aims to test real-life skills. The reading that you do outside the classroom will help you become a better reader.
- Improve your scanning skills. This is reading a text quickly in order to find specific information.
- Learn to use key words to scan a text for specific information or details. Use advertisements, notices, and texts from letters, emails, magazines, newspapers, websites, and leaflets to practise this skill.
- Work with a partner: remove some of the words from a text, and then use key words in the sentences to help you decide what information is missing.

</td></tr>
</table>

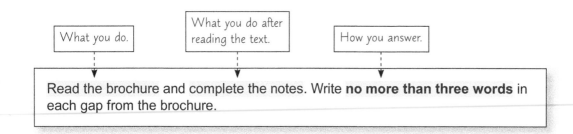

What you do.	What you do after reading the text.	How you answer.

Read the brochure and complete the notes. Write **no more than three words** in each gap from the brochure.

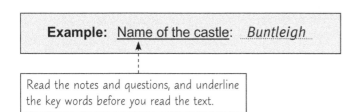

Example: <u>Name of the castle:</u> *Buntleigh*

Read the notes and questions, and underline the key words before you read the text.

Section 8: Write correspondence

What is being tested?

Section 8 tests your ability to write a piece of correspondence.

What do you have to do?

Write an email, a formal or information letter, a post card or a note based on information given in Section 7. There is one text to write (50–70 words). There is a "tolerated" word limit of 40–77 words for Section 8. If the response is below or over this limit, you will automatically score 0 for the section.

Strategy

- Read the instructions very carefully.
- Check the task instructions to find out what you are writing and who you are writing to. You need to understand the purpose of the correspondence.
- Cover all the bullet points in your writing. Avoid writing too much about one and not enough about the others.
- Highlight the parts of the text in Section 7 that you could use to plan the content of your answer. You will need to refer to the text in Section 7, usually by summarising the main idea and/or commenting on it. In either case, you should use your own words as far as possible. The *Writing Guide* on pages 54-60 provides some help with this.
- Leave a few minutes at the end of the task to check through your work.
- Check your writing for the accuracy of your grammar and spelling, and that you have written between 50 and 70 words.

Preparation tips

- Work on improving your vocabulary by reading and noting down words and expressions you might use to write on topics such as family, hobbies, work, travelling and shopping.
- Learn how to plan your writing and what information you need to include. Practise using linking words. Use the *Writing Guide* on pages 54-60, which also gives you useful language you can use.
- Understand what kind of mistakes you make in your writing; try to improve those areas. Build a list of your errors (for example, by using a piece of past work marked by your teacher) as a guide.
- Practise checking through your work for spelling errors. Work with a partner to discuss content and organisation, and to correct each other's language errors.

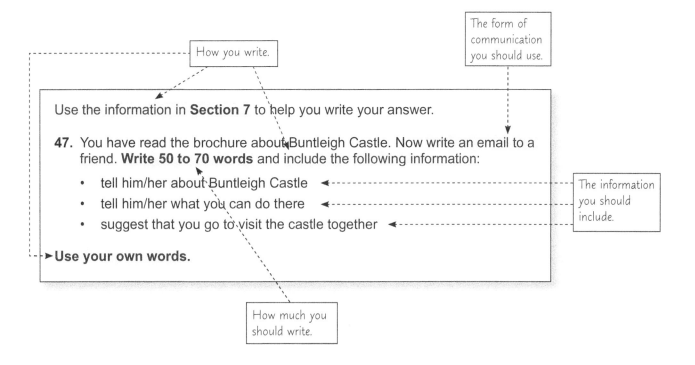

How you write.

The form of communication you should use.

Use the information in **Section 7** to help you write your answer.

47. You have read the brochure about Buntleigh Castle. Now write an email to a friend. **Write 50 to 70 words** and include the following information:

- tell him/her about Buntleigh Castle
- tell him/her what you can do there
- suggest that you go to visit the castle together

► **Use your own words.**

The information you should include.

How much you should write.

Section 9: Write text

What is being tested?

Section 9 tests your ability to write a short text based on pictures.

What do you have to do?

Write a piece of writing from a choice of two options. Each option consists of a series of three images. The form of the response may be a short story, a description or a diary entry. There is one text to write (80–100 words). There is a "tolerated" word limit of 48–110 words for Section 9. If the response is below or over this limit, you will automatically score 0 for the section.

Strategy

- Read the introduction to the task and choose one option.
- Think quickly about the vocabulary you need to use to make sure you know enough words to write your answer.
- Think what type of writing you need to produce (a story, description or diary entry) and what tense(s) you need to use.
- Try to use linking words to link your sentences.

- Leave a few minutes at the end of the task to check through your work.
- Check that your grammar and spelling is correct.

Preparation tips

- Use the *Writing Guide* section of the book on pages 54–60.
- Work with a partner. Find a picture from a book or magazine and write a story or a description. Work with your partner to discuss the content and to correct each other's language errors.

> What you should do.

> How much you should write.

48. Choose **one** of the topics below and write your answer in **80–100 words**.

   A Jessie is your friend. He had some trouble walking his dog. Look at the pictures and write a short story about how he solved his problem.

> Think about the topic and make a short plan of what you want to write.

Section 10: Sustained monologue

What is being tested?

Section 10 tests your ability to speak continuously about matters of personal information and interest.

What do you have to do?

Speak continuously about a familiar topic for up to one minute. The examiner might ask you some follow-up questions to encourage you to continue talking. The questions focus on regular and routine activities. This section of the test lasts 1.5 minutes.

Strategy

- You need to talk about a familiar topic on your own for about one minute.

- If you don't, the examiner may ask you some questions to encourage you to talk. Listen to the examiner's questions very carefully before giving an answer.

- Try to give an answer which is more than just a few words.

- Remember that it is quite natural to pause very briefly for thought when you are speaking.

Preparation tips

- Make sure you are familiar with the task: what the examiner will do and how long the section is.

- Practise talking about yourself with other students on a range of different topics. Choose a topic, for example, shopping, and ask each other different questions.

- Practise talking for about one minute on a topic, with a classmate timing you.

- Work on building your vocabulary on a range of familiar topics.

- Practise listening carefully to questions and thinking about the topic before giving an answer.

How long you need to speak on your own.

In this section you will speak on your own for about a minute. Listen to what your teacher/examiner asks. Your teacher/examiner will ask one of the main questions below, and the follow-up questions if necessary.

Preliminary prompt 1:   *Do you enjoy music?*

Main prompt 1:   *Tell me the type of music you enjoy listening to.*

Follow-up prompts:
- *Where do you usually listen to music?*
- *Do you know any songs in English?*
- *What's the most popular music in your country?*
- *How often do you buy CDs?*

What the examiner will ask you.

Section 11: Discussion

There is no Section 11 in PTE General Level 1.

Section 12: Describe picture

What is being tested?

Section 12 tests your ability to speak continuously about a picture.

What do you have to do?

Speak continuously about a picture that the examiner presents to you for up to 1 minute. Then answer any follow up questions that the examiner might ask you. This section of the test lasts 2 minutes.

Strategy

- The examiner will present you with a card and will ask you to describe a picture.
- Try to talk about the picture for about one minute.
- Describe the picture using sentences rather than words.
- Look at the picture carefully; say what you see in the picture, who you think the people in the picture are, where they are, and what they are doing/wearing.
- The examiner may ask you some follow-up questions about the picture to encourage you to speak more.

Preparation tips

- Make sure you are familiar with the task: what you are expected to do, what materials you will be given, what the examiner will say and how long the task is.

- Practise describing a picture with other students. Ask each other different questions. Here is some useful language you can use:

What is in the picture

This picture shows …

There is/there are …

I can see …

What is happening

The boy is … ing

The people are …-ing

They are …-ing

Where in the picture

On the right / On the left …

Under / Near / Behind / Next to / In front of …

If something is not clear

Maybe it's a …

He might be a …

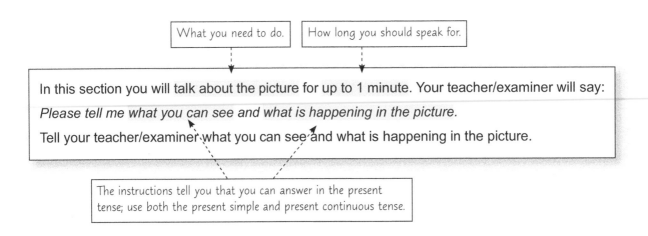

What you need to do. How long you should speak for.

In this section you will talk about the picture for up to 1 minute. Your teacher/examiner will say:

Please tell me what you can see and what is happening in the picture.

Tell your teacher/examiner what you can see and what is happening in the picture.

The instructions tell you that you can answer in the present tense; use both the present simple and present continuous tense.

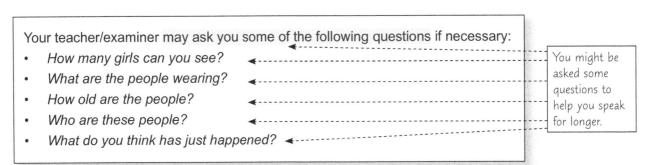

Your teacher/examiner may ask you some of the following questions if necessary:

- *How many girls can you see?*
- *What are the people wearing?*
- *How old are the people?*
- *Who are these people?*
- *What do you think has just happened?*

You might be asked some questions to help you speak for longer.

Section 13: Role play

What is being tested?

Section 13 tests your ability to perform and respond to language functions appropriately.

What do you need to do?

Take part in a role play with the examiner using a role card with information and instructions. This section of the test lasts 1.5 minutes.

Strategy

- The examiner will present you with a card.
- Listen to the examiner very carefully.
- You will be given 15 seconds to read the instructions and prepare.
- Try to think of some ideas based on the information on the card.
- If you are not sure what to do, ask the examiner.
- The examiner will say who should start the role play. For example, if the examiner is going to start he/she would say: *Ready? I'll start.*
- You don't need acting skills to take part in the role play. Take time to understand the situation and just be as natural as possible.

Preparation tips

- Make sure you are familiar with the task: what you are expected to do, what the examiner will say, what materials you will be given, and how long the task is.
- Work with a partner. Practise different language functions such as asking for directions/ information, giving information, apologising and responding to an offer in different situations.
- Improve your vocabulary. Learn words that are related to different routine matters (for example, buying a ticket, making an appointment). This will help you to speak without too many pauses when it is your turn to talk.

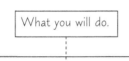

In this section you will take part in a role play. Your teacher/examiner will explain the situation.

What your role is and what you are doing.

Test taker's card

You are on a football field. You invite your friend to play on your team. The examiner is your friend.

- Greet your friend.
- Say you want him/her to play on your football team.
- Tell him/her why you want him/her to play on your football team.
- Invite him/her to play on your football team tomorrow.

The examiner's role.

What you should do in the role play.

Writing Guide

Introduction

In Pearson Test of English General, there are two sections which assess your writing skills.

Section 8

In Section 8 you are asked to write a piece of correspondence. This may take the form of an email, a letter, a postcard or a note.

What you have to write will always be a response to the text you read in Section 7. For example, you may be asked to write a postcard to a friend giving them information about the place you are visiting. You will need to refer to the text in the previous section. You should use your own words as far as possible, not simply copy parts of the original text. Exactly what you need to include is indicated by three bullet-pointed instructions.

The word limit in this section is **50–70 words**. You may well find that the biggest problem is not that this is a lot of words, but that, once you start writing, it is not enough to include everything that you want. For this reason, it is important to express yourself concisely.

Section 9

This section is a writing task in which you need to write a short text based on a series of three pictures. What you are asked to write can take various forms. It might be a story, a blog or a diary entry based on the pictures.

There will be a choice of two tasks. The topics will be related to two of the themes of the test, so there may be ideas you can use in other sections of the test, but, again, you should use your own words. The word limit is **80–100 words**.

General advice

There are specific tips in the *Exam Guide* section of this book. Below are some more general pieces of advice relating to writing in general and in the Pearson Test of English General.

- Always be aware of the reader: the person or people that you are writing for. This will have an effect on both the content and the style of what you write. Generally speaking, an informal, more conversational style is best for letters and emails to friends.

- Don't pre-learn large sections and long phrases, for example, introductions, and try to fit them into your writing, whatever the topic. Firstly, it often looks unnatural and is usually easy for the examiner to notice. Secondly, it is often a waste of words: if you use up a lot of your word limit on "decoration", you might find you have no room left to say anything useful.

- Make a short plan of what you want to write. In this way, your writing will be clearer and better organised. Paragraphing makes the organisation of your writing clear. Linking words will also help to do this, but, if the writing is well organised, it does not need very many. It is probably enough to have two or three basic words or phrases for various purposes. For example, use *and* or *also* for adding extra information, and *but* for showing contrast. The most important thing is that you understand how to use them.

- When you have finished writing, check what you have written for mistakes, especially the ones you make under pressure and which you would get right if you thought about it. Try to be aware of the kinds of mistake you tend to make frequently.

- Your writing will be marked for how well it performs the task as well as for the language, so make sure you cover all the points required by the question and bullet points.

Blog entry

Model answer

You have read an article about your town. Now write a blog entry about your town.
Write **50–70 words** and include the following information:

- what your favourite place is in your town
- say what you can do there
- say what you like about it

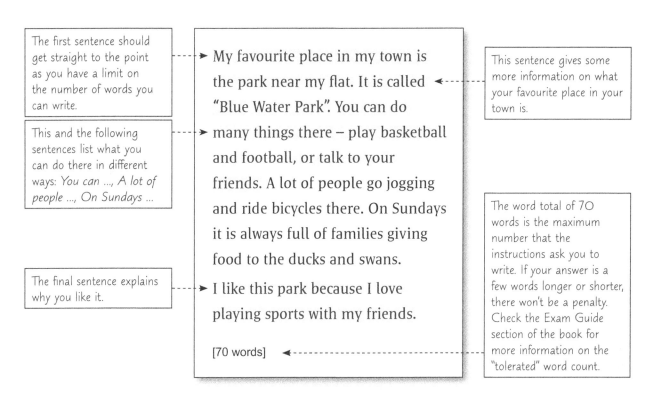

The first sentence should get straight to the point as you have a limit on the number of words you can write.

This and the following sentences list what you can do there in different ways: *You can ..., A lot of people ..., On Sundays ...*

The final sentence explains why you like it.

> My favourite place in my town is the park near my flat. It is called "Blue Water Park". You can do
>
> many things there – play basketball and football, or talk to your friends. A lot of people go jogging and ride bicycles there. On Sundays it is always full of families giving food to the ducks and swans.
>
> I like this park because I love playing sports with my friends.
>
> [70 words]

This sentence gives some more information on what your favourite place in your town is.

The word total of 70 words is the maximum number that the instructions ask you to write. If your answer is a few words longer or shorter, there won't be a penalty. Check the Exam Guide section of the book for more information on the "tolerated" word count.

Writing about what you like/don't like

I really like/don't like …
I enjoy/love …
I don't like/enjoy …
My favourite place is …

Explaining

I am happy because …
I like it because …
It was great because …

Listing or giving examples of activities

You can …
My friends and I go/do/play …
A lot of/Some people …
On Sundays …
At the weekend(s) …
Most days …
Sometimes …

Postcard

Model answer

You are on a class trip to London. Now write a postcard to your friend.
Write **50–70 words** and include the following information:

*   describe the city
*   name one place you visited
*   explain why you liked it

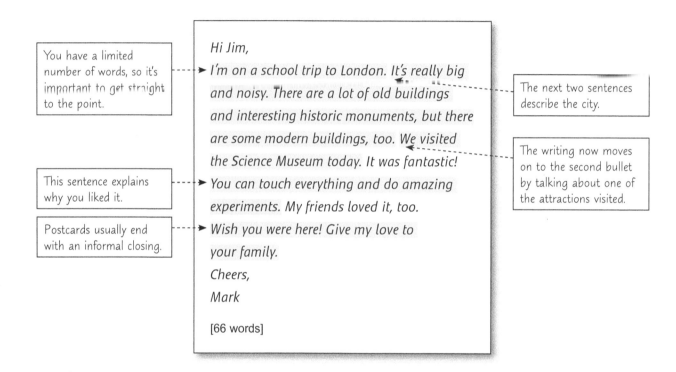

You have a limited number of words, so it's important to get straight to the point.

Hi Jim,

I'm on a school trip to London. It's really big and noisy. There are a lot of old buildings and interesting historic monuments, but there are some modern buildings, too. We visited the Science Museum today. It was fantastic!
You can touch everything and do amazing experiments. My friends loved it, too.
Wish you were here! Give my love to your family.
Cheers,
Mark

[66 words]

The next two sentences describe the city.

The writing now moves on to the second bullet by talking about one of the attractions visited.

This sentence explains why you liked it.

Postcards usually end with an informal closing.

Useful language

Describing things

It is/was a very big …
There are/were some/many/
a lot of …
It was interesting/fantastic/amazing.

Describing feelings

I had a lovely/great time.
It is/was fun/exciting.
I loved/liked/enjoyed …-ing …

Letter: thanking

Model answer

You received a letter with a gift from one of your friends for your birthday. Now write a letter to thank your friend. Write **50–70 words** and include the following information:

- thank your friend for the gift
- describe what you did on your birthday
- ask him/her to go camping with you

Thank your friend for the present straightaway. This is usual in a letter of thanks and you have a limited word count, so it's important to get straight to the point of the letter.

These sentences cover the second bullet point on what you did on your birthday.

Hi Josh,

Thank you very much for the lovely photo book you sent me. I loved it, the photos are really nice. I didn't have a birthday party this year. I just went out for dinner with some friends. We watched a movie after dinner. I am going camping in April with a few friends, would you like to join us? It would be fun.

Let me know

Tom

[69 words]

This sentence starts by introducing the fact you are going camping. It gives the date and who you are going with.

The second half of the sentence deals with the third bullet: inviting your friend to go with you, using *would you like …?*

Useful language

Thanking
I just wanted to thank you for …
Thank you so much for …
I really appreciate it.

Inviting
I hope you can …
Would you like to … ?

Email: invitation

Model answer

You have received an email from your friend who is visiting your country. Now write an email to your friend. Write **50–70 words** and include the following information:

- invite him/her to stay with you
- suggest what you can do
- say why he/she should come

After a short opening, the email starts off with the invitation to your friend.

This sentence gives interesting concerts as a reason why your friend should come. The email also uses some expressions to try to make your friend want to come: *We'll have a lot of fun!, I really hope you can come.*

Dear Mark,

How are you? I'd like to invite you to come and stay with me this summer when you come to England. We'll have a lot of fun! We can go sailing or how about visiting some historic cities, like Bath or York? There are always interesting concerts there in the summer.

I really hope you can come.

Let me know what you think!

Best,

Alex

[67 words]

This suggests what you can do together.

Different grammatical structures are used to make suggestions: *We can ..., how about ...?*

Useful language

Opening

Dear James,

Hi, James,

It's always good to hear from you.

Thanks for your letter.

How are you?

I hope you're well.

Inviting

I hope you can …

Would you like to … ?

I just wanted to invite you to …

Closing

Yours

Best wishes

Write soon

See you

Thanks again

Hope to hear from you soon

Love

Email: giving information

Model answer

You have read an email from your friend who is coming to stay with you for a holiday. Unfortunately, you cannot pick him/her up from the airport. Now write an email to your friend. Write **50–70 words** and include the following information:

- explain why you can't pick him/her up
- describe the person who will pick him/her up
- tell him/her where the person will be waiting

This sentence apologises first of all and then explains why you can't go.

Hi Mark,

I'm really sorry, but I can't meet you at the airport tomorrow because I've got a bad cold and I have to stay in bed. My friend Stella will pick you up. She's quite tall, her hair's long and blonde, and she's got a bright red coat. She's going to wait for you in front of the flower shop at the airport.

See you soon!

Alex

[68 words]

The description of the person includes their name, what they look like (height, length and colour of hair) and what they will be wearing.

Here, the email explains where the person will be waiting.

Explaining
I can't do it because …
I am happy because …
I like it because …
It was great because …

Apologising
I'm really sorry, but …
I'm so sorry that I can't …

Short story

Model answer

Last weekend you stayed with your Uncle Tom's family. Look at the pictures and write a description of what happened for your diary.

Write your answer in **80–100 words**.

The first sentence gives background information and introduces your story.

Use linking words, such as *and* or *but*, to connect your sentences.

Describe things.

> Last weekend I stayed with my Uncle Tom. After breakfast, Josh and I helped him to wash his car. It was fun. In the afternoon, we all went to a park near their house. We took their dog Digger with us, too. The weather was very nice and we played football. I really enjoyed it.
>
> In the evening, we went out for a meal in the city. He took us to a very nice restaurant. The meal was very delicious. We talked about different things. I had a very good weekend. Next weekend, Josh is going to stay with us.
>
> [100 words]

Describe the events in a logical order.

Describe people's feelings.

Finish off your story with an ending. Don't just stop writing when you reach the top of the word limit.

Useful language

Giving information
My sister/uncle lives/works in …
My father/brother/cousin is …
My brother played/plays …
We worked/cleaned/ate/drove …

Describing things
a very big building
a very good/nice time
a big/small house/flat/park
It was very exciting/fantastic/beautiful.

Describing feelings
We enjoyed/liked/loved …
We had a great time.
I/We/They enjoyed/liked …-ing

Audioscript

Practice Test 1

Section 1

Narrator: You will have ten seconds to read each question. Listen and put a cross (✗) in the box next to the correct answer, as in the example. You have ten seconds to choose the correct option.

Example

Listen to the man and woman talking. What does Anna want to buy?

Man: Are you going into town this morning, Anna?

Girl: I want to spend my birthday money.

Man: What are you going to buy? A bag or another CD?

Girl: No! I want to get a new dictionary.

Narrator: The correct answer is B.

Number 1

Listen to the people speaking. What is the woman's job?

Man: What do you do?

Woman: I'm a taxi driver. Before that I worked in a café.

Man: Did you work part-time when you were at school?

Woman: Yes, in a shop.

Narrator: **Number 2**

Listen to the conversation. Which is Elizabeth's bike?

Man: Is this Elizabeth's bike? With the basket?

Woman: Well, her bike has got a basket. But it's at the back, not the front.

Narrator: **Number 3**

Listen to the voicemail. Who is the message for?

Woman: Oh, hello. It's Mrs. Williams here. I'm calling because John isn't very well today, so I'm keeping him at home. Can you phone me later about his homework? Thank you.

Narrator: **Number 4**

Listen to the man and woman speaking. How is the man going to the station?

Man: Excuse me. Can I get a bus to the railway station?

Woman: Not from here. But it's only ten minutes on foot.

Man: No. I'll call a taxi. These bags are too heavy to carry.

Narrator: **Number 5**

Listen to the man. Which is the correct picture?

Man: I have three sisters. Mary is very tall with long black hair. Gill is also tall, but her hair is blond. My little sister Amy has blond hair, too. She's my favourite!

Narrator: **Number 6**

Listen to the conversation. What's the boy doing this afternoon?

Boy: Mum? I'm not playing football this afternoon.

Woman: Oh. Are some of the team on holiday?

Boy: No. The weather's too bad.

Woman: Yes, it's raining again. Well, you can help me in the house instead.

Narrator: **Number 7**

Listen to the man speaking. What is Mr. Hammond's job?

Man: Mrs Jones, my name is John. I'm your dentist's secretary. I'm sorry, but Mr Hammond is ill, and is not working today. Please call back to make a new appointment.

Narrator: **Number 8**

Listen to the man speaking. Where is the sandwich?

Man: Tom, Dad here. There's a sandwich for your lunch. It's on the table in the dining room. There's also some soup on the cooker or some salad in the fridge.

Narrator: **Number 9**

Listen to the woman speaking. What is Julia going to do that morning?

Woman: Julia, Dad and I are going to go for a walk in the hills today. Can you clean your room after lunch? Oh, and don't forget your tennis match at eleven o'clock this morning.

Narrator: **Number 10**

Listen to the woman. Which platform is the train to York leaving from?

Woman: The eight fourteen train to York is now leaving from platform six. This is a change from platform two. Please go to platform six for the eight fourteen to York.

Section 2

Narrator: **Number 11**

You will hear a recording about pets. Listen to the whole recording once. Then you will hear the recording again with pauses for you to write down what you hear. Make sure you spell the words correctly.

Woman: Tomorrow there is a programme about pets. It is about rabbits and what they eat. Please tell your children so that they can watch it.

Narrator: Now listen again and write down your answer.

Woman: Tomorrow there is a programme about pets. // It is about rabbits // and what they eat.// Please tell your children // so that they can watch it.

Section 3

Narrator: **Numbers 12–16**

You will hear a voicemail message. First, read the notes below, then listen and complete the notes with information from the voicemail. You will hear the recording twice.

Man: Oh, hi, Angie. It's Nick here. Thanks for offering to help us move to the new flat. We're now moving next Thursday, not Tuesday. I know you're free on both those days. So, can you come to our old flat at half past eight please – no sorry, make that eight o'clock. There's so much to do! Bring some newspapers with you – lots of them, please! We'll need it for wrapping things up. Tom's packing everything – he's good at that. You and I can clean the flat. You know, for the new people. I hope that's OK with you. I've got a new phone number by the way. It's oh seven eight four nine, one six double nine two. Thanks again, Angie.

Narrator: Now listen again.

Numbers 17–21

You will hear a telephone message. First, read the notes below, then listen and complete the notes with information from the telephone message. You will hear the recording twice.

Man: Hello. This is Tom. I'm at work. Can you phone the vet for me and make an appointment? They're called The Ark and the number is oh one two seven one, three nine eight double three two. I think they're open this morning from half past eight till half past twelve. If they ask, it's about my dog, Marley – that's M-A-R-L-E-Y. If you can get an evening appointment, that's best for me. Oh, and if it's this evening, can you send me an email, please? Thanks a lot. See you later.

Narrator: Now listen again.

That is the end of the listening section of the test. Now go on to the other sections of the test.

Practice Test 2

Section 1

Narrator: You will have ten seconds to read each question. Listen and put a cross (**X**) in the box next to the correct answer, as in the example. You have ten seconds to choose the correct option.

Narrator: **Example**

Listen to the man and woman talking. What does Anna want to buy?

Man: Are you going into town this morning, Anna?

Girl: I want to spend my birthday money.

Man: What are you going to buy? A bag or another CD?

Girl: No! I want to get a new dictionary.

Narrator: The correct answer is B.

Number 1

Listen to the people speaking. What was Ben doing last night?

Girl: Ben, did you watch that documentary about body language last night?

Boy: I saw it was on, but I was busy with my homework. What was it about?

Girl: What different body moves mean.

Narrator: **Number 2**

Listen to the woman. Who is she describing?

Woman: He really enjoys his job. He really enjoys his job. He <u>is</u> very happy when he can help <u>young</u> people, but sometimes he finds it hard when students behave badly.

Narrator: **Number 3**

Listen to the man speaking. What is next to the Majestic?

Man: We're meeting at six in front of the Majestic and then going to a restaurant. The Majestic is the cinema next to the pharmacy, not the one near the bookshop.

Narrator: **Number 4**

Listen to the man talking. Who is he talking about?

Man: She started when she was very young. She used to sit around and think about her stories. She didn't draw the pictures herself, she just wrote everything down and someone else did the pictures.

Narrator: Number 5

Listen to the people talking. Where are they?

Man 1: Good morning. How are you feeling?

Man 2: Much better this morning. It isn't so windy and the sea is nice and flat.

Man 1: Yes, it's a perfect day. We should arrive in Cyprus by lunchtime.

Narrator: Number 6

Listen to the woman speaking. What's her job?

Woman: We have a sale on at the moment. These are all from last year, but the style is still very popular. Hmmm, I think this dark green one would suit you. What a lovely colour!

Narrator: Number 7

Listen to the conversation. Where is Tom?

Mum: Tom, can you help me in the kitchen, please?

Tom: Mum, I'm watching football now. What would you like me to do? I want to take a shower, too. Can I do it after that?

Narrator: Number 8

Listen to the man. Where do they go on holiday?

Man: We always go on holiday to the same place. It's a cottage on the east coast, miles away from the nearest town. It isn't even on a bus route!

Narrator: Number 9

Listen to the conversation. What is Josh using?

Lucy: Hey, Josh, who are you texting?

Josh: Hi, Lucy. I'm not texting anyone. I'm playing a game.

Lucy: Oh, right. I don't like playing games on my phone. I don't know how you do it.

Narrator: Number 10

Listen to the man speaking. What is he describing?

Man: It's very close to the beach so it's easy to get to. You can exchange money there and you can check in or out twenty-four hours a day, which is perfect if you have a flight in the middle of the night.

Section 2

Narrator: Number 11

You will hear a recording about Ann's grandfather. Listen to the whole recording once. Then you will hear the recording again with pauses for you to write down what you hear. Make sure you spell the words correctly.

Woman: My grandfather was a doctor. He worked in a small clinic near his house for many years. I sometimes went to see him after school.

Narrator: Now listen again and write down your answer.

Woman: My grandfather was a doctor. // He worked // in a small clinic near his house // for many years. // I sometimes went to see him // after school.

Section 3

Narrator: Numbers 12–16

You will hear an advertisement. First, read the notes below, then listen and complete the notes with information from the advertisement. You will hear the recording twice.

Woman: The new Edge Hill Shopping Centre is now open. With 120 shops, 6 restaurants, 5 cafés, a cinema and a children's play area, the Edge Hill Shopping Centre is the biggest shopping centre in this area. We also have a "learning centre" where children from five to eighteen can read books. Children under twelve must have an adult with them at all times. The learning centre is free to use, but you must join first.

The shopping centre is open from 7 a.m. until 10 p.m. from Mondays to Saturdays and from 9 a.m. to 8 p.m. on Sundays. There is also a free shopper's bus which leaves the Edge Hill railway station every half hour.

Narrator: Now listen again.

Numbers 17–21

You will hear a presentation about the Eiffel Tower. First, read the notes below, then listen and complete the notes with information from the presentation. You will hear the recording twice.

Tour guide: Here we are in the centre of Paris standing right in front of the Eiffel Tower, one of the most famous monuments in the world. Almost seven million tourists visit this tower every year. Today, it is over 125 years old! The tower is 320 metres tall; its base is square and is 125 metres long on each side. The tower is painted every seven years. And guess how much paint they use each time? Fifty tonnes of paint! There are 1,665 steps! If you want a challenge, you can climb the stairs to the second level. From the second floor you can go up in the lift and travel 180 metres up to the third level. Tickets can be purchased online to avoid the long queues.

Narrator: Now listen again.

That is the end of the listening section of the test. Now go on to the other sections of the test.

PTE General: Top 20 Questions

1 How many marks are needed to pass the exam?
To pass the exam you need a score of 50 or above.

2 Do I have to pass each paper in order to pass the exam?
No, each paper doesn't have a pass or fail mark. Your overall grade comes from adding your marks in both the Written and Spoken papers.

3 Are marks taken off for wrong answers?
No. This means that, if you are not sure, you should always try to choose the answer you think is best – you might be right.

4 Am I allowed to use a dictionary in the exam?
No.

5 Generally, in the exam, if I am not sure about an answer, can I give two possible answers?
No. If there are two answers, one of them is wrong; you will not get a mark. So you must decide on one answer to give.

6 How many times will I hear each recording in the Listening sections?
In Section 1, once. In Section 2, you will hear the recording twice, the second time with pauses giving you time to write down word-for-word what is heard. In Section 3, you will hear each recording twice.

7 In Listening Section 2, what happens if I misspell a word?
All answers need to be correctly spelt, so you will lose marks.

8 In Listening Section 1 and Reading Section 5, what should I do if I am not sure which picture is correct?
Check them again, there is only one correct picture. Sometimes, the pictures might look similar, but there will be some small differences that will help you find the correct answer.

9 In Listening Section 3, should I use the words I hear in the recording?
You can expect to hear some of the words in the recording. When you are completing sentences, you should check that the completed sentence with your answer inserted makes sense and is grammatically correct.

10 In Listening Section 3, what happens if my answer is too long to fit in the space on the answer sheet?
Most answers are single words, numbers or groups of two to three words. If you think the answer is longer, then it is probably incorrect.

11 In Reading Section 6, should I write a complete sentence in answer to the questions?
You should write only the word or words that answer the question.

12 In Reading Section 7, what happens if I write words that are not from the article?
The words should come from the text.

13 In Reading Section 7, what happens if I write more than three words in a gap?
Answers are one to three words. If you think the answer is longer, it is probably incorrect.

14 In Writing Section 8, what happens if I don't write about all the points listed with bullet points (•)?
You should write about all the bullet points. The examiners are looking to see if you can provide the right information and good language.

15 In Writing Section 8, can I copy words/text from the text in Section 7?
You can use parts of the input text in Section 7 to plan the content of your answer, but you need to use your own words and ideas as much as you can.

16 In Writing Sections 8 and 9, what happens if I write too few or too many words?
The word count is an important guide. It tells you how much to write when doing the task. There are tolerated ranges for each section. Your teacher will be able to guide you on these. Make sure you stay within the relevant range and use about the right number of words in your answer. Plan your time so that you write about the right amount and have time to check what you have written. You will not lose score points if you stay within the tolerated word limits.

17 What happens if I make a spelling mistake in the Writing sections?
All spelling must be correct; spelling is one of several things that the examiner considers when deciding what mark to give you.

18 For the Speaking paper, is it a good idea to prepare what I am going to say in Section 10?
It is, of course, good to prepare well for the exam. But you cannot know exactly what the examiner will ask beforehand, so you must listen very carefully to the examiner and make sure you answer the questions relevantly.

19 In Speaking Section 10, what happens if I cannot talk for one minute on my own?
The examiner will ask you some follow-up questions to encourage you to talk more about the topic. Listen carefully to the examiner's questions before giving an answer.

20 In Speaking Section 13, how much time will I have to prepare for the role play?
You will have 15 seconds to prepare. Use this time to develop ideas and questions based on the test taker's card.